The Adventures of Mr D.

Jennifer Seidl

Cornelsen

Cornelsen English Library

Verlagsredaktion
Dr. Blanca-Maria Rudhart

Umschlaggestaltung
Heike Börner, dia

Titelbilder
Michael Fleischmann
Dundee City Council/Tayside Image Bank

Illustration
Michael Fleischmann

Gestaltung & technische Umsetzung
Anna Bakalovic und Annika Preyhs, Berlin

www.cornelsen.de

1. Auflage, 1. Druck 2006

Alle Drucke dieser Auflage sind inhaltlich unverändert und können im Unterricht nebeneinander verwendet werden.

Druck: Druckhaus Berlin-Mitte

ISBN-13: 978-3-464-31180-6
ISBN-10: 3-464-31180-5

Inhalt gedruckt auf säurefreiem Papier, umweltschonend hergestellt aus chlorfrei gebleichten Faserstoffen.

Contents

Chapter 1

"Eight thirty-five. Oh, no! I´m late again," said Sally Parker in a worried voice as she looked at her watch. "This is the second time this week. And no time for breakfast again. Oh, well ... Now, where´s my bag and where are all the exercise books?"

Sally Parker took her bag from behind the sofa, put on her jacket and left the house in a hurry. "Have I got my keys?" she thought.

But what was that? As she closed the front door, she heard a noise from the bushes. What was it? She listened and looked.

"Oh, you poor thing," she said gently as she saw a thin, hungry cat on her doorstep. The cat looked up at her with big, green eyes. "What are you doing here? You´re hungry, I can see.Well, just wait here, little cat. Don´t go away."

Suddenly there was a bowl of milk and a few small chicken pieces on the doorstep – and a very happy cat.
"What will Mr McCraig say this time?" Sally Parker thought as she hurried down the road. "Just two minutes before the first lesson starts. But that poor cat. I had to feed him."

She walked faster and turned the corner into Park Road. She could see the entrance to Dundee Park School now. Almost there at last. Was Mr McCraig at the school entrance again?

Was he watching who came late? No, he wasn´t there this time. That was lucky.
Miss Parker ran to the teachers´ room, took off her jacket, then hurried to her classroom. Nobody saw that she was late. Lucky again ... Was this her lucky day?

"Good morning, class!" she said as she closed the classroom door behind her. But what was that? She felt something soft and warm near her feet. She looked down. And there were those big, green eyes again – the cat.
"Miaow, miaow!"

"Oh! A cat! A cat! Great! Is it your cat, Miss?" shouted Toby. "Can we stroke him?"
"Come here, cat. What´s your name? Have you got a name, Mister Cat?" added Toby´s twin sister, Lisa. "Has he got a name, Miss?"

Miss Parker was still standing by the door. She didn´t know what to say. How did the cat get into the school? She left him on her doorstep – and now here he was in her classroom with all her children. "No animals in classrooms. That´s a school rule," she thought. "What will Mr McCraig say? Oh, dear ... I´m in really big trouble this time. What can I do? I must talk to the children."

"Quiet, please. Quiet. Well, as you can see, we´ve got a cat in our classroom. He isn´t my cat. I found him outside my house this morning. He was hungry, so I fed him. He followed me to school, but I didn´t see him. And now, here he is! You know the school rule: No animals in classrooms. He must be a stray, but we can´t keep him. When Mr McCraig finds out that we´ve got an animal in the classroom ... well, he won´t be very happy. So what can we do with the cat? Have you got any ideas?"

"Can´t you keep him, Miss? Can´t he live with you?" asked Toby. "He likes you."

"Well, I live alone and I´m here in school all day. Cats like company. I think he needs a family with children. He´s a nice, little cat and he needs a good home. Perhaps some of your parents or your neighbours can give him a home."

"My dad doesn´t like cats," said Sam.

"We´ve got neighbours with a big dog," said Lucy.

"And my mum says our flat is too small for a pet," added Katy.

"We´ve already got three pets – a tortoise, a budgie and a hamster," said Emma.

"And I´ve got lots of fish. Cats like fish, but I don´t think my fish will like the cat. Sorry, Miss," shouted Ranjit from the back of the room.

"Well, I know it´s difficult, but perhaps you can all ask at home. We can talk in our lesson again tomorrow. Okay?"

"And where can the cat sleep tonight, Miss?" asked Toby. "Please don´t take him to the animal home."

"Well, no… er… I don´t know. We´ll see."

The cat wasn´t listening. He was busy looking round the classroom. Was there a sofa for his sleep?

Chapter 2

"Please, Miss Parker, can I go to the toilet?" came a voice from the back of the class.

"All right, Ranjit. But hurry. We have to start our lesson now. Let me see. Where are we in our book? Yes, page 64 in the middle. And be quiet, please. No more noise now. Shhh!"

Ranjit left the room – and the cat left the room too, but nobody saw him. The children were all busy with page 64.

"This is a really big house," he thought. "I must look round and explore."

The school was quiet now. The cat walked up the stairs and looked round. Then he walked down again and looked round. Nobody saw him. So many rooms, so many doors. He looked for an open door. He was still hungry. Perhaps there was a kitchen somewhere.

He soon came to the science lab. The door was open a little and the room was empty, so he went in – and saw lots of interesting things. There were cupboards and long tables. There were lots of chairs – but no sofa. There was a big sink and lots of bottles of water in different colours – red water, blue water, pink water, yellow water …

"Ah!" thought the cat. "This must be the kitchen. Now, where´s the milk? And which door is the fridge door?"

The cat opened some cupboard doors and pulled out some boxes and bottles, too. Somehow some of the bottles fell on the floor – and the water ran out ...

"But where´s the fridge with the fish and the milk? It must be here somewhere. And what´s that? Where´s all that smoke coming from? And what a terrible smell! I think I have to look somewhere else," thought the cat. "This is a really strange kitchen."

Suddenly there was a noise from outside the room. A very loud bell was ringing. Hundreds of feet were running down the corridor. Loud voices were shouting happily. The cat was frightened. "What´s happening? Lots of people are coming. They´re looking for me. Quick! I must hide," he thought.

There was a door at the back of the science lab. It was open, just a little. It was dark inside the room, but there was nowhere else to go. The cat went in. "It´s quiet here. I´m safe now. Nobody can see me. Nobody can find me," he thought. The cat waited and waited until the noise stopped.

It was the morning break. The children were outside now. They were talking and laughing. Some were playing football. Others were eating sandwiches or phoning on their mobiles.

The cat was still in the biology store room.

"Where am I? What´s in here?" he wondered. He pushed the door open from inside and some light came in. Yes, now he could see better. He looked round. Lots of old things, but no food. Just old things. Then suddenly he looked up to the top shelf. Aaaaagh! Two big, yellow eyes were looking down at him! There was a gigantic bird in the cupboard! Quick! Out of here! Run! Run!

"Will anybody see me? Can I get away?" thought the cat ...

Chapter 3

The cat went down some stairs into another room, a very big, bright room with a shiny floor. It was empty and quiet: no children, no tables and chairs. But there were some interesting things to climb on. He was in the gym. He jumped up onto the beam and walked along it slowly from one end to the other. Then he jumped even higher onto the parallel bars – oops, careful. He jumped from one piece of apparatus to the other. It was easy for the cat and lots of fun.

The basketball net looked interesting. It´s nice to be high up, where you can see everything.
But – oh, dear – the ring of the basket was very narrow, and somehow the cat fell off it – and landed in the basketball net. He was hanging in the net with his legs through the holes. He couldn´t jump out.

Just then the big door of the gym opened and three children came in with a teacher. It was Toby, Jamie and Lisa from Form 8SP with the PE teacher, Mr Hill.
"Okay, you three. You can help me with the ... What was that noise? Did you hear it? What was it?"
"What noise, Sir? I didn´t hear anything," said Toby. "What kind of noise did you hear?"
"Well, like a baby – or an animal – like a cat. Yes, like a cat!"

"A cat? Oh, no!" thought Lisa. "Is our cat in here? Where is he? I can´t see him."
"Miaow, miaow," came a voice from one end of the gym – from up above.

Four pairs of eyes looked up at the basketball net …

"Miaow, miaow …" said a little voice again.

"There´s a cat up there! Or am I dreaming? Is there really a cat up there, in the basketball net?" said Mr Hill.

The children were very quiet. Nobody spoke. They just looked.

Lisa had a red face. Toby wanted to laugh – but he didn´t.

"How did the cat get into school? And how did it get in the basketball net?" said Mr Hill in an excited voice.

"And how can we get him down?" asked Lisa in a very quiet voice – and with a very red face.

Toby and Jamie didn´t know what to say. The three children looked at each other with eyes and mouths wide open.
"That´s our cat up there. We´ll be in big trouble. And Miss Parker will be in very big trouble," thought Lisa.

Then lots of other children ran into the gym – the rest of Form 8SP.
"There´s our cat again!" shouted one of the boys. They all ran to the basketball net and looked up at the frightened cat. Then they started to laugh and shout loudly. "Jump, cat! Jump!"

"Shh! Quiet!" shouted Mr Hill. "Our cat? You said *our* cat, Sam? Is it your cat? What do you know about it? "
"Nothing, Sir. Nothing. Let´s get him down. He´s frightened."
"You´re Form 8SP, Miss Parker´s form. Does she know about the cat? Does she know that you brought a cat to school? Well, does Miss Parker know?"

All the children were quiet now. Nobody spoke. Nobody wanted to answer Mr Hill´s questions.
"Ah, I see," said Mr Hill after a long silence.
"Nobody knows about the cat. Nobody. Well, let´s get the cat out of the net. Then I´ll talk to Mr McCraig. Somehow I don´t think he will be very pleased."
"Miaow, miaow, miaow ..." said a small voice from up above.
"Right, Form 8SP. I´ll get the caretaker first. Stay here – and be quiet! No noise!" shouted Mr Hill as he left the gym.

Then the students talked loudly together.

"How did he get up there? What shall we do? What can we say? We can´t tell Mr McCraig that the cat came to school with Miss Parker. He´ll be very angry."

"Well, let´s get the cat down before Mr Hill comes back. I´ve got an idea. Come on, Toby. Stand on my shoulders! We can get him down and let him out. Then Mr McCraig won´t find him and everybody will forget about it," said Jamie. "Right. Help us, Lisa!"

Toby tried to stand on Jamie´s shoulders and reach the cat, but he fell down three times ...
"Ouch! My knee!" called Toby as he lay on the floor for the third time. "Sorry, cat. We can´t help."

The cat was still in the net when Mr Hill returned with the caretaker. He was carrying a ladder. The caretaker wasn´t in a good mood. But Mr Briggs was never in a good mood. He didn´t like noisy children. And he certainly didn´t like cats in basketball nets ...

Mr Briggs climbed up the ladder and took the cat out of the net. The children watched quietly. Then Mr Briggs climbed down the ladder and put the cat on the floor. "Now don´t let me see you here again!" he shouted, as the cat ran out of the gym like a shot. "Cats. Who needs cats?" Mr Briggs went on, as he took his ladder and left the gym.

The cat ran outside. That was enough excitement for one morning.

Chapter 4

In the lunch break the students were in the canteen. Some had their sandwich boxes with them, others were eating school dinner. There was lots to talk about. The students in Form 8SP were telling their friends about the cat in the basketball net ... Their friends were laughing and asking lots of questions.

"How exciting! You´re lucky! Why don´t cats come into our classroom?" said Ben from 8AK. "It´s better than Maths lessons!"
"How did the cat get into the basketball net? That´s brilliant!" added Jason from 9DW. "And where is he now? Can we see him? Why can´t we have a cat?"

Miss Parker was eating a sandwich in the teachers´ room. Suddenly a voice from behind said, "Miss Parker, I´d like to speak to you. Come to my room, please." It was Mr McCraig.

"Oh, dear. What´s wrong now? What does he want to talk to me about? He didn´t see me this morning when I arrived late. But he doesn´t sound very friendly," thought Sally Parker as she put down her cup of tea. "Oh, I think I know ... I´m in trouble again. And I thought this was my lucky day ..."
"Yes, of course, Mr McCraig," she answered with a nervous feeling in her stomach.

"Close the door, please, Miss Parker."

She closed the door of Mr McCraig´s room behind her and stood in front of his desk. She didn´t sit down.

"Please sit down. Yes, well, Miss Parker, I heard that you had a cat in your classroom this morning. You´re new here, but you must know that it´s against the school rules. No animals in classrooms. Can you explain what happened, please?"

"Yes, well ... er ... that is, no, you see ...", Miss Parker began.

"Miss Parker, did you have a cat in your classroom this morning? Yes or no?"

"Well, yes, but ..."

"And did the cat make a terrible mess in the science lab? And did it cause a big disturbance in your form´s PE lesson this morning?"

"Oh, really? I didn´t know that. I´m very sorry, but ..."

"Yes, I´m sure you are very sorry, Miss Parker. There´s a mess in the science lab. And ask Mr Hill what happened in the gym!"

"Well, it isn´t my cat, Mr McCraig. I didn´t know that he followed me to school. I found him at my door. He was very hungry, so I fed him."

"I understand, Miss Parker. This is your first year as a teacher and you have a lot to learn, but you must know that it´s against school rules to take animals into classrooms. If teachers don´t keep the rules, what can we expect from our students? Students are not allowed to bring their pets with them. This is a school, not a zoo," continued the headmaster.

"Yes, of course, Mr McCraig."

"But that isn´t all. You´re often late for the first lesson. You were five minutes late on Monday. Your class is usually noisy when you´re not there. And now this trouble with an animal in school. It isn´t good enough. I must warn you. Please don´t let this happen again."

"It won´t happen again, Mr McCraig, and I am very sorry about the trouble in the science lab – and in the gym."

"Oh, no. This is certainly not my lucky day," thought Sally Parker as she left the headmaster´s room. "I wonder where the cat is now ..."

Chapter 5

It was five o´clock in the afternoon. Toby and Lisa Ashton were having tea with their mum. Toby and Lisa were 12-year-old twins. They both had blond hair, but otherwise they were quite different. Lisa was the quiet twin, sometimes a little shy. Toby was usually the noisy twin. He talked a lot. He always had lots to say about everything. But today he was quiet. The twins wanted to talk to their mum about the cat, but they didn´t know how to start. Both children were nervous. Lisa looked at Toby and knocked his leg with her foot under the table. Her eyes said, "Go on, Toby, say something!"

"Mum, something really nice happened in school today," Toby began nervously.

"Really? Well, I´m sure you´re going to tell me, so go on," said Mrs Ashton as she poured tea into the cups.

"A cat came into our classroom in the first lesson. Miss Parker was a bit late and he followed her to school. Suddenly, there he was! Miss Parker didn´t know what to say. The cat was hungry, so I gave him some ham from my sandwich. He´s thin, but he´s really sweet and he´s clever too."

"Hungry cats are always clever," said Mrs Ashton. "But perhaps he´s got a home."

"No, he doesn´t look like a house cat," Lisa went on.

"That´s the problem. We need a good home for him because our teacher can´t take him. She lives alone and she´s in school all day. Cats don´t like to be alone all day. She can´t leave him in the house and she can´t leave him on the streets."

"And she told us that there´s a big dog next door," added Toby.

"We know you and dad like animals, and we´re sure you like cats. We would love to have a cat," continued Lisa.

"And this cat costs nothing," said Toby. "We can have him for free. And you can have lots of fun with a cat. They´re very clean animals, they don´t usually make a mess and ..."

"All right, all right, you two. But a pet always costs money and a pet means responsibility – not only for parents but also for children. A pet isn´t just a toy to play with and have fun with. You can´t just put it back in the box when you don´t want to play. And there are other things to think about. A pet sometimes has to go to the vet. It needs a nice basket. It has to have proper food. And what happens to the cat when we go on holiday in summer? And what happens to the cat when grandma visits us – she doesn´t like cats. I agree that a

pet is fun, but it isn´t always easy. You must talk to dad when he comes home. But I don´t think he will agree," said Mrs Ashton as she poured more tea into the cups.

Toby and Lisa just looked at each other. They didn´t say anything. They didn´t feel very hopeful now. Toby looked at his watch.
"Dad will be home soon, I think."

After a while Lisa said, "Mum´s right. An animal is a big responsibility and not a toy. But think of the cat hunters, bad people who take cats from the streets and sell them to laboratories for experiments. That is terrible. Just imagine, our Mister Cat in a laboratory with .... Oh, no. I don´t even want to think about that. We must find a safe home for him. Let´s hope that dad is in a good mood ..."

But Mr Ashton was not in a good mood. He came home and just sat down in the chair. He wasn´t very cheerful and he didn´t talk much. He looked sad and worried. He had problems.
So Toby and Lisa didn´t tell him about the cat ...

Later, when the children were upstairs, Mr and Mrs Ashton talked quietly together in the kitchen with the door closed. When Toby went to the kitchen for a drink, he heard something through the door, something about dad´s job, no summer holiday and no new TV ...

Chapter 6

"About the cat, Miss," Toby began in the English lesson on the next day. "We asked at home, but I´m afraid we can´t take him."

"All right, Toby. I understand. That´s okay," answered Sally Parker quietly.

"My mum said yes but my dad said no," added Jason.

"My grandma would like a cat, but she lives in London," said Nicole. "That´s a long way from Dundee."

"Well, thank you all for asking," answered Sally Parker. I know that it´s difficult. I didn´t see the cat this morning. Perhaps he´s got a home already. Let´s hope so. Now, let´s start our lesson."

The day passed without the cat. It was soon 3.30. The bell rang and the schoolday came to an end. Some of the students from Form 8SP stayed at school for different clubs and activities, but for Sally Parker the schoolday was over.

On her way home she stopped at the supermarket. She bought bread and some nice slices of turkey for her sandwiches for school the next day. Turkey sandwiches with tomato and a bit of mayonnaise were her favourites.

Home at last. At the front door she put down her shopping bag and looked for her keys.

"Miaow, miaow ..." came a voice from the bushes.

"Cat! You´re here again. My students talked about you in school today. I heard about you from the headmaster too.

You´re a little troublemaker. You did some bad things. Well, I can´t leave you outside. So come in."

Sally Parker opened the door and the cat went in first. He looked into all the rooms. He found the kitchen particularly interesting ...
"I expect you´re hungry. Just wait a few minutes and I´ll give you something to eat." Sally Parker took off her coat and put her shopping bag in the kitchen.
The cat sat and waited near the shopping bag. When she took out the turkey the cat said "Miaow, miaow" quite loudly.
"Yes, that´s it. That´s for me," he thought. She cut a slice of turkey into small pieces and put it on a plate. The cat ate the meat with appetite. He wanted more, so she gave him more. Then she thought about her sandwiches for school, "Oh, well. Just tomato and mayonnaise tomorrow ..."

Sally was worried about the cat. He was a street cat. She couldn´t lock him in her house all day. Her students couldn´t take him. She phoned the animal home, but they were full. Then she phoned all her friends. But nobody could take the cat ... "What will happen to the cat if he doesn´t find a home? He´ll live on the streets – until the cat hunters take him ..."

Sally and the cat spent the evening together on the sofa in the living room. The cat sat on an old cushion. They watched TV. The cat liked that. Sally liked it too. She stroked the cat and talked to him. She soon forgot the trouble with Mr McCraig.

Before she went to bed she remembered something – the goldfish bowl.

"Where shall I put it? I can´t leave it in the living room. Yes, I know, the bedroom – on top of the cupboard, perhaps. It´s a funny place for a goldfish bowl – but it´s the safest place." She closed the bedroom door too.

When Sally woke up the next morning, she immediately thought about the cat. Was everything okay? Yes, there he

was in the kitchen, near the fridge door. Sally Parker gave him the rest of her turkey for breakfast – and made her tomato sandwiches for school. "I´m going to school now, but you really can´t go with me this time. You did some bad things last time – and I was in big trouble. You must stay here in the house. But it´s my short day at school, so I´ll be back at lunchtime. Now, be good, please! Just go to sleep."

Sally Parker left the house in a hurry, as always. "He´s quite a wild one," she thought, as she locked the front door. "He´s alone now. I wonder what he´ll do …"

Chapter 7

Sally Parker arrived home just after one o´clock.

"Hello, cat! I´m back. Where are you?" she said as she put her bag and her shopping on the hall table. The cat came out of the kitchen and rubbed against her legs. "Ah, there you are. Are you okay?" Oh, yes. The cat was quite okay.

Then the phone rang. It was her mother.

"Surprise, surprise! I´m at the station. Can you pick me up, please? I know that today is your short day. I have a few bags to carry."

Sally still had her coat on, so she decided to go to the station immediately. She thought about her mother. "Mother doesn´t like cats. Why does she have to visit me today – when I´ve got a cat in the house? What shall I do?"

"Cat, my life is suddenly difficult with you – and it isn´t good! Sorry, but I must leave you in the house again."

As she closed the front door, deep in thought, she didn´t notice that the cat left the house too. He was very quick.

The cat didn´t like closed doors. He liked his freedom. He was a cat, not a dog. He didn´t need a master. He didn´t need rules for things you must do and things you mustn´t do. A cat likes to do just what it wants. A clever cat even likes the streets. On the streets there´s something new every day – new places, new dustbins, new friends. But on the streets there are also dangers – hunger, traffic, big dogs, unfriendly people, cat hunters …

The cat disappeared down the road and was on his way to school again.

This time the cat didn´t go into the school building. He explored the schoolyard.
At one end of the yard there was a house with a high wall round it. Cats like walls. You´re the king on top of a wall. You can lie in the sun too. Yes, a wall is a good place.
The cat climbed up a small tree, and from the tree he jumped onto the wall. The cat liked to see everything.

Well, there were lots of things on the other side. There was a small garden with some flowers. There was a shed full of things for the garden. There was an old bike. There were buckets and boxes, bottles and old boots for the garden. There was a dustbin too. "Ah, now that´s interesting," thought the cat.

It was the caretaker´s house.
The cat walked along the wall, looked round, then quickly jumped down onto the dustbin. But the dustbin – and the cat – crashed to the ground with a loud noise ... "Miaow!"
The caretaker ran out of the house, saw the rubbish on the ground – and the cat on the wall. "It´s that cat again!" he shouted. "What a terrible mess ! Go away and don´t come back! You´re just a troublemaker. We don´t need any cats here!"

Mr Briggs had a broom in his hand and he was angry. But the cat was safe on the high wall. The caretaker couldn´t reach him. Then suddenly a big dog came running round the corner and barked loudly at the cat.

"Trouble again," thought the cat as he ran along the wall. He didn´t know that a dog lived in the house too. But the cat was in safety now, up on his wall, so he watched and listened …

Chapter 8

Mr Briggs lived alone in his house. His wife was dead. He wasn´t a young man and the work in the school was sometimes not easy for him. He wasn´t an unfriendly man, but he sometimes had problems with the headmaster, who really wanted a younger caretaker. That made Mr Briggs discontented and sometimes bad-tempered. He didn´t have much company, only his dog, Monty. Monty was a good friend. Mr Briggs liked dogs. You can talk to dogs when you´re lonely. They seem to understand you. They always welcome you when you come home, and they also know what they mustn´t do. You can train dogs. But cats? No. Mr Briggs didn´t like cats.

Every day Mr Briggs walked round the school and the yard. He repaired things. He cleaned things. He painted things. He cut the grass and the bushes. He kept the schoolyard tidy.

Today was his day to check the heating, so he took his ladder and walked down the steps to the cellar. He unlocked the door of the boiler room with his keys. The boiler room was dark and noisy. Mr Briggs turned on the light and walked in. Suddenly he stopped. There was a funny smell. What was it? It smelt like gas. Was it gas? Oh dear. That could be dangerous. Dundee Park was quite an old school, and the heating pipes were also quite old. Was there a leak somewhere? He went over to a little window at the other side of the room and opened it. Fresh air. That was better. But it was windy outside and the open window caused a strong draught. A door banged somewhere. Mr Briggs started to check the pipes. He thought he could find the leak. Just a small thing perhaps. But the smell got stronger. "No, this isn´t a job for me. I must phone the gas company or the fire brigade. There´s something wrong here," he thought. He took his ladder and walked back to the door quickly, but it was closed. Yes, of course, the draught and the bang. He felt in all his pockets for his keys. But they weren´t there. Oh, no! Perhaps they were still in the lock, on the other side of the door … He was trapped!

He banged on the door with his fists. "Help! Help! Get me out!" he shouted. "Help me, please!" But there was nobody in the cellar. The students and teachers were all in their classrooms. Nobody could hear him.

He was afraid. He already felt a little dizzy from the gas. He tried to walk back to the window. He held on to the pipes and almost reached the window. "Help! Help!" he called weakly. "Please help me! I´m in here!" But he tripped and fell on the floor. As he fell, he hit his head against the wall. And now there he lay, unconscious …

Chapter 9

The wind was blowing dry leaves across the schoolyard. The cat was lying in the sun, but he was watching the leaves and the insects and the birds. Perhaps there was a mouse somewhere too. Yes, there was! There! A mouse! What luck!

The cat jumped towards the mouse, but the mouse was faster. The cat ran after it towards the school building, but it disappeared into a hole near the wall. So the cat sat next to the hole and watched, waited and sniffed ...

The cellar window wasn´t far away. Perhaps the mouse was down there. As the cat walked towards the window he smelt a strange smell. Cats can smell much better than people. He looked down into the boiler room. Perhaps the mouse was hiding there. Suddenly he saw that someone was lying on the floor. And that smell …

The cat didn´t jump down into the cellar. He walked backwards, away from the window. At first he did nothing. He just stood there, looked and listened. It was very quiet. There was nobody in the schoolyard. But then he ran into the school building. He sensed that something was wrong. He knew the way to 8SP´s classroom. He scratched on the door and miaowed as loudly as he could. Suddenly Lisa opened the door. "Mister Cat! What are you doing here? You can´t come into school. Miss Parker isn´t here. We´ve got History now with Mr Hill. You mustn´t scratch on the door. Stop it! Go away, please!"

Lisa closed the door and tried to concentrate on Henry the Eighth. But the scratching started again. This time Mr Hill opened the classroom door. "Cat! Miss Parker´s friend. Go away! You´re a troublemaker. There´s nothing for you here." But the cat didn´t go away. He miaowed and scratched at Mr Hill´s trousers excitedly.

"He wants something," said Lisa. "Or perhaps he´s trying to tell us something."

"No. He´s hungry again, I expect. But we can´t feed him. If we feed him, he´ll come again and again," said Mr Hill, who wasn´t really a cat fan.

The cat scratched and miaowed, walked away a few steps, then turned back to Mr Hill and the children, scratched and miaowed again and again.
"He wants to show us something," said Toby, who was now outside the classroom with half the class.
"Look. He´s trying to pull at my trousers," added Jamie. "I´m going to follow him."
"Yes, me too. Is it okay, Mr Hill? Can we go with the cat and see what he wants?"
"We´re having a History lesson. We can´t follow the cat around in the middle of it. How can I explain it to the headmaster if he sees us? The cat got Miss Parker into trouble – and now me. No."
"But please, Mr Hill. It won´t take long – and it could be important, " continued Toby.

"Okay, okay. We´re wasting time. Toby, Jamie, Lisa, go with the cat and be back in five minutes! If you aren´t back, you´ll all get extra homework," said Mr Hill, now in a bad mood.

The cat ran out of the school building. Toby, Jamie and Lisa ran after him.
"Where´s he taking us?" shouted Lisa to the others.
"I don´t know. Let´s go there and see!" answered Toby.

They followed the cat along the side of the school. Several heads in the classrooms turned to watch. Then the cat ran round the corner to the back of the building. The children followed him, to a small cellar window …

"There´s nothing here. Just a window. Silly cat! Do you want us to find mice in the cellar for you?" said Jamie, who didn´t understand all the excitement.
But Toby walked to the window, got down on his knees and looked down into the boiler room ...

"Oh, no! There´s somebody down there. He´s lying on the floor. I think it´s Mr Briggs. And there´s a funny smell. It could be gas. Quick! We must get help!"

Lisa and Jamie stood there with mouths wide open. "Lisa, run to Mr McCraig and tell him to phone for an ambulance! And fetch Mr Hill! Jamie, you come with me! I hope we aren´t too late ..."

Chapter 10

The three students ran back into the school. Toby ran down the steps to the cellar, but he wasn´t sure which was the right door.

Lisa ran to Mr McCraig´s room. She knocked, but she didn´t wait for an answer. Mr McCraig was sitting at his desk and he looked at Lisa in great surprise as the door suddenly opened.

"Sorry, Sir, but Mr Briggs is unconscious in the cellar and there´s a funny smell. We have to get him out. Please phone for an ambulance. There must be a gas leak too. Is it dangerous, Sir? Toby and Jamie are down there."

The headmaster looked very worried, but he didn´t ask questions. He phoned for an ambulance and for the fire brigade immediately.

At the same time Jamie ran to the classroom to fetch Mr Hill.

"Mr Hill, please come quickly. Mr Briggs is lying on the floor in the boiler room. He must be unconscious. His head´s bleeding. And there´s a gas leak. Lisa´s just telling Mr McCraig. Sir, please do something. Toby´s down there too!"

"Oh, no! Okay, Jamie. Calm down. You wait here. I´ll try to get Mr Briggs out. Stay here and don´t let Lisa or any other students go down there. Okay?"

"All right, Sir," said Jamie, but he followed Mr Hill into the cellar. His friend was down there ...

Toby found a door which said *Keep Out* on it – and the key was in the lock. What luck! Toby wasn´t really brave, but he knew that somebody must help Mr Briggs. There was no time to lose. Toby held two paper tissues over his mouth and nose and opened the door. He saw Mr Briggs on the floor, but first he opened another small window. He knelt on the floor. "Are you okay, Mr Briggs? Can you hear me? Help is coming but we have to get out of here. Can you get up?"

But Mr Briggs didn´t answer. Was he still alive? Toby could smell the gas and knew that he had to get Mr Briggs out – fast. He put his right arm under the caretaker´s head and shoulders and tried to move him. But it was no good. So he tried to pull the unconscious man towards the door. But he wasn´t strong enough. Where were the others? Where was help? Was anybody coming? Toby felt very alone. For the first time in his life he was really afraid. Would help come in time …?

Chapter 11

"Toby! Where are you?" shouted a voice from the door.

"We´re here, near the window," replied Toby. It was Mr Hill – and Jamie.

"Are you okay, Toby? There´s a strong smell of gas down here."

"Yes, I´m fine, Sir. But I´m very glad you´re here."

"Okay. Now, we have to move quickly. I´ll lift him under his arms. Jamie, you take one leg and Toby the other. One, two, three … "

As they were carrying Mr Briggs out of the cellar they heard loud voices upstairs. Suddenly Mr McCraig appeared.

"Is he all right? The ambulance and the fire brigade are on the way. I´ll help Mr Hill now, boys. You run upstairs and show the ambulance men where we are. Are you sure you´re both okay?"

Then it all happened very quickly. The paramedics arrived and carried Mr Briggs into the ambulance on a stretcher. At the same time the fire brigade arrived. Mr Hill spoke to one of the men, then he climbed into the ambulance with Mr Briggs. Mr McCraig spoke to one of the firemen. Toby, Jamie and Lisa watched. As the ambulance drove off Toby asked,

"Is he going to be all right, Sir?"

"Well, we can´t be sure," replied Mr McCraig. "We have to wait and see. Mr Hill will phone me from the hospital. Now, you three, tell me how you found Mr Briggs. How did you know about the accident? What were you doing in the boiler room …?"

"Well, Sir, you see ... Do you remember the cat who ...?"

The firemen quickly found the gas leak and repaired it. One of the men said, "It was lucky that you called us so soon ..."

The cat sat in the sun in the schoolyard and licked himself. What an interesting day. So much to see ...

Chapter 12

"The hospital phoned to say that Mr Briggs is going to be fine. He can come home this afternoon," said Mr McCraig at Assembly the next morning. All the students clapped and cheered at the good news.

"And I must say, it was thanks to the cat – who seems to like our school. Lisa and Toby Ashton and Jamie MacDougal from 8SP told me all about the rescue – and I´m sure you all know the story now too," he went on. Everybody smiled.

In the morning break Mr McCraig said, "I thought your cat was just a troublemaker, Miss Parker. So did Mr Hill. We were wrong. Thanks to the cat Mr Briggs is alive and well. It was certainly his lucky day. I´m very glad now that the cat followed you to school ..."

Mr Hill and Miss Parker looked at each other and smiled.

"Here he is! Here´s our hero!" shouted Toby, as he and lots of other students came running up with the cat. Everybody wanted to stroke him. Life was so good ...

"You´re a real hero, and now you´re our form cat," said Lisa.

"No, he isn´t your form cat. He´s our school cat!" shouted Jason from 9DW.

"Okay. But he hasn´t got a name. He must have a name." Lisa looked at the others. "Any ideas?" she asked.

"Well, if he´s our school cat, we could call him Dundee Park or Dundee!" suggested Jason from 9DW.

"No! Dundee Park is a silly name for a cat," said Lisa. "But what about Mister D? Let´s call him Mister D!"
"Brilliant, Lisa!" shouted Jamie. "Yes, I like that. That´s great. He´s our Mister D! Okay, everybody? Yes? Okay!"

"Well, I´ve got some good news for Mister D," continued Mr McCraig. "I spoke to Mr Briggs on the phone just a few minutes ago. He said he didn´t like cats before, but now he says he wants to take Mister D to live in his house with him and Monty. He´ll be safe and happy. He´ll have friends – and his freedom. Mr Briggs also said that 8SP can come to tea next week. There will be chocolate cake and ice cream for everybody."
"Hooray for Mr Briggs – and Mister D!" shouted the students.

Just then the bell rang and the students went off to their classes.
"Goodbye for now!" thought Mister D as he jumped up onto his wall again. "I´ll be back …!"

Vocabulary

A

above [ə'bʌv] oben
accident ['æksɪdənt] Unfall
(to) **add** [æd] hinzufügen
again and again [ə'gen] immer wieder
against [ə'genst] gegen
(to) **agree** [ə'griː] zustimmen
air [eə] Luft
alive [ə'laɪv] am Leben
almost ['ɔːlməʊst] fast
alone [ə'ləʊn] allein
along [ə'lɒŋ] entlang
ambulance ['æmbjələns] Krankenwagen
angry ['æŋgri] verärgert
apparatus [æpə'reɪtəs]: **piece of apparatus** *hier:* Turngerät
(to) **appear** [ə'pɪə] erscheinen
as [æz] als, während

B

bad-tempered [bæd'tempəd] schlecht gelaunt
back (n.) [bæk] Rückseite
backwards ['bækwədz] rückwärts
(to) **bang** [bæŋ] zuschlagen; hämmern
(to) **bark** [bɑːk] bellen
basket ['bɑːskɪt] Korb
beam [biːm] *hier:* Schwebebalken
became [bɪ'keɪm]: (to) **become, became** werden
(to) **bleed** [bliːd] bluten
boiler room ['bɔɪləruːm] Heizraum
boring ['bɔːrɪŋ] langweilig
brave [breɪv] tapfer
bright [braɪt] hell
broom [bruːm] Besen
bucket ['bʌkɪt] Eimer
busy ['bɪzi] beschäftigt

C

(to) **calm down** [kɑːm daʊn] sich beruhigen
canteen [kæn'tiːn] Kantine
caretaker ['keəteɪkə] Hausmeister
cat hunter ['kæt ˌhʌntə] Katzenfänger
(to) **cause** [kɔːz] verursachen, herbeiführen
cellar ['selə] Keller
(to) **cheer** [tʃɪə] jubeln
cheerful ['tʃɪəfl] fröhlich
(to) **clap** [klæp] Beifall klatschen
closed [kləʊzd] geschlossen
(to) **come running** gelaufen kommen
company ['kʌmpəni] Gesellschaft
corridor ['kɒrɪdɔː] Gang
(to) **crash** [kræʃ] stürzen
cushion ['kʊʃn] Kissen

D

danger ['deɪndʒə] Gefahr

dangerous ['deɪndʒərəs] gefährlich
dead [ded] tot
(to) **decide** [dɪ'saɪd] (sich) entscheiden
(to) **disappear** [ˌdɪsə'pɪə] verschwinden
discontented [dɪskən'tentɪd] unzufrieden
disturbance [dɪs'tɜːbəns] Störung
dizzy ['dɪzi] schwindlig
doorstep ['dɔːstep] (Tür-) Schwelle
dry [draɪ] trocken
dustbin ['dʌstbɪn] Mülleimer

E

each other [iːtʃ 'ʌðə] einander
entrance ['entrəns] Eingang
even ['iːvn] sogar
excited [ɪk'saɪtɪd] aufgeregt
excitement [ɪk'saɪtmənt] Aufregung
exciting [ɪk'saɪtɪŋ] aufregend
(to) **expect** [ɪk'spekt] erwarten
experiment [ɪk'sperɪmənt] Experiment
(to) **explain** [ɪk'spleɪn] erklären
(to) **explore** [ɪk'splɔː] erkunden/ auf Entdeckung gehen

F

fault [fɔːlt]: **It isn´t your fault.** Es ist nicht deine Schuld.
felt: (to) **feel, felt** sich fühlen
fire brigade ['faɪə brɪˌgeɪd] Feuerwehr
fist [fɪst] Faust
free: for free [friː] kostenlos/ umsonst
freedom ['friːdəm] Freiheit
fright [fraɪt] Schreck
frightened ['fraɪtnd] verängstigt
front door [frʌnt 'dɔː] Haustür
funny ['fʌni] komisch/seltsam

G

gently ['dʒentli] sanft
gigantic [dʒaɪ'gæntɪk] gigantisch
glad [glæd] froh/erfreut
ground [graʊnd] Boden
gym [dʒɪm] Turnhalle

H

hall [hɔːl] Flur
headmaster [hed'mɑːstə] Schuldirektor
heating ['hiːtɪŋ] Heizung
(to) **hit** [hɪt] schlagen
hole [həʊl] Loch
hopeful ['həʊpfl] hoffnungsvoll
(to) **hurry** ['hʌri] eilen
in a hurry in Eile

I

(to) **imagine** [ɪ'mædʒɪn] sich vorstellen
immediately [ɪ'miːdiətli] sofort
important [ɪm'pɔːtnt] wichtig

K

keep [kiːp] behalten
keep the rules die Regeln einhalten
knelt [nelt]: (to) **kneel** [niːl] knien
knock [nɒk]: stoßen; klopfen

knock against sth. gegen etw. stoßen
knock sth. **over** etw. umstoßen

L

lab [læb] *(Abkürzung)*
laboratory [lə'bɒrətri] Labor
ladder ['lædə] Leiter
leaf [li:f] pl. **leaves** [li:vz] Blatt
leak [li:k] Leck
(to) **leave** [li:v] lassen
(to) **lick** [lɪk] lecken; **lick himself** sich lecken
light [laɪt] hell
(to) **lock** [lɒk] einsperren
lock (n.) [lɒk] Türschloss
lonely ['ləʊnli] einsam
(to) **lose** [lu:z] verlieren
lucky day [ˌlʌki 'deɪ] Glückstag

M

master ['mɑ:stə] Herrchen
(to) **matter** ['mætə]: **It doesn´t matter** Es macht nichts.
mess [mes] Durcheinander, Schmutz
mood [mu:d]: **in a good/bad mood** gut/schlecht gelaunt sein
(to) **move** [mu:v] sich bewegen

N

narrow ['nærəʊ] schmal
nervous ['nɜ:vəs] nervös
net [net] Netz
news (sing.) [nju:z] Neuigkeiten
no good: It was no good. Es nützte nichts. Es hatte keinen Sinn.
noisy ['nɔɪzi] laut
(to) **notice** ['nəʊtɪs] bemerken
nowhere else nirgendwo anders

O

oh dear! [əʊ 'dɪə] ach je!
over ['əʊvə]: **be over** zu Ende sein

P

paper tissue ['tɪʃu:] Papiertaschentuch
parallel bars [ˌpærəlel 'bɑ:z] Barren
paramedic [pærə'medɪk] Sanitäter
particularly [pə'tɪkjələli] besonders
(to) **pass** [pɑ:s] vergehen/vorbeigehen
(to) **pick** [pɪk] sb. **up** jdn. abholen
pipe [paɪp] Rohr
pleased [pli:zd] erfreut
pocket ['pɒkɪt] Tasche (Hose, Jacke)
(to) **pour** [pɔ:] einschenken/gießen
proper ['prɒpə] richtig

Q

quite [kwaɪt] ziemlich

R

(to) **reach** [ri:tʃ] erreichen
(to) **remember** [rə'membə] sich an etw. erinnern
rescue ['reskju:] Rettung

responsibility [rɪˌspɒnsəˈbɪlɪti] Verantwortung
(to) **return** [rɪˈtɜːn] zurückkommen
(to) **rub** [rʌb] reiben
rubbish [ˈrvbɪʃ] Müll/Abfall
rule [ruːl] Regel

S

safe [seɪf] sicher
safety [ˈseɪfti] Sicherheit
(to) **scratch** [skrætʃ] kratzen
(to) **sense** [sens] spüren
shed [ʃed] Schuppen
shiny [ˈʃeɪni] glänzend
shot [ʃɒt] Schuss
shy [ʃaɪ] schüchtern
side [saɪd] Seite
silence [ˈsaɪləns] Schweigen
sink [sɪŋk] Waschbecken
slice [slaɪs] Scheibe
smell [smel] Geruch
smile [smaɪl]: **smile at** sb. jdn. anlächeln
(to) **sniff** [snɪf] schnuppern
somehow [ˈsʌmhaʊ] irgendwie
stairs [steəz] Treppe
still [stɪl] noch
store room [ˈstɔː ruːm] Abstellkammer
strange [streɪndʒ] merkwürdig
stray [streɪ] Streuner
stretcher [ˈstretʃə] Tragbahre
strict [strɪkt] streng
(to) **stroke** [strəʊk] streicheln
(to) **suggest** [səˈdʒest] vorschlagen
sure [ʃʊə] sicher
surprise [səˈpraɪz] Überraschung

T

thought [θɔːt]: Gedanke; **deep in thought** in Gedanken versunken
towards [təˈwɔːdz] in Richtung
toy [tɔɪ] Spielzeug
traffic [ˈtræfɪk] Verkehr
trapped [træpt] eingesperrt
(to) **trip** [trɪp] stolpern
trouble [ˈtrʌbl] Ärger; **be in (big) trouble** (viel) Ärger bekommen
troublemaker [ˈtrʌblˌmeɪkə] Unruhestifter
turkey [ˈtɜːki] Putenfleisch
twin [twɪn] Zwilling

U

unconscious [ʌnˈkɒnʃəs] bewusstlos
unfriendly [ʌnˈfrendli] unfreundlich
upstairs [ʌpˈsteəz] oben

V

vet [vet] Tierarzt

W

(to) **warn** [wɔːn] warnen
(to) **waste** [weɪst] verschwenden **waste time** Zeit vergeuden
Watch out! [ˌwɒtʃ ˈaʊt] Pass auf!
(to) **wonder** [ˈwʌndə] sich fragen
(to) **worry** [ˈwʌri] sich Sorgen machen
worried [ˈwʌrɪd] beunruhigt/unruhig

Y

yard [jɑːd] Hof

Names

Briggs [brɪgz]
Dundee [dʌn'diː]
Jamie ['dʒeɪmi]
Jason ['dʒeɪsn]
Lisa ['liːzə]
McCraig [mə'kreɪg]
MacDougal [mək'duːgl]
Ranjit ['rændzɪt]

Questions and Activities

Chapter 1

1 What do you know about Miss Parker? Write three or more things.
Ideas: *lives in ..., a teacher at ..., late, Form 8SP, kind to animals*

2 What did Miss Parker talk about with her students?
Words: *cat, school rule, home, parents and neighbours*

3 Find a title for chapter 1.

4 NOW YOU
- Have you or your friends or neighbours got a pet?
- Draw a picture of your favourite pet and write about it.

Chapter 2

1 Where did the cat go? What happened there?
Words: *explore, look for the kitchen, science lab, bottles, mess, biology store room.*

2 Find a title for chapter 2.

Chapter 3

What´s missing? Find the words in the text.

1 It was a big, bright room with a shiny floor. The cat was in the ___ .

2 Mr Briggs is the school __________ .

3 Toby and Jamie wanted to get the cat out of the basketball net. Toby stood on Jamie´s __________ .

4 Toby fell on the floor three times. He hurt his ____ .

5 Mr Briggs came into the gym. He was carrying a ______.

6 The cat ran out of the gym like a ____ .

Chapter 4

1 At lunchtime the students talked to their friends about the cat.
Work in groups of five students. Write a short scene with Toby, Jamie, Lisa, Ben and Jason. Then learn your part and act the scene.

2 Where was Miss Parker at lunchtime? Who wanted to speak to her? What did they speak about?

3 Find a title for chapter 4.

Chapter 5

1 Toby, Lisa and their mum were having tea. What did they say? Write a short scene. Then act the scene.

2 What do you think will happen to the cat? Will Mr Ashton say yes or no? Why?

Chapter 6

1 Where is Dundee? Is it in England, Ireland, Scotland or Wales?

2 Why was Sally Parker worried about the cat?

3 NOW YOU
Talk about animal homes in class. Who lives there and why?
How can we help? Write a few sentences.
Ideas: *stray dogs and cats, cages, food, helpers, volunteers* (Freiwillige)

4 Sally Parker and Form 8SP are afraid of cat hunters and animal experiments. *Animal Aid* is the UK´s biggest and oldest animal rights (Tierrechte) group. Look at their website: *http://www.animalaid.org.uk* .

5 Work in groups. Collect information and pictures about animal homes and animal rights groups. Then make a class poster. Which poster did the class (or you) like best? Why?

Chapter 7

1 Why did Sally Parker go to the station?

2 Where did the cat go?

3 What dangers are there for stray cats on the streets?

4 Why do cats like walls?

Chapter 8

What´s missing? Find the missing words in the text.

1 Mr Briggs sometimes had problems with the ___________.

2 Mr Briggs lived in his house alone because his wife was ____.

3 He went into the cellar because he wanted to check the ________.

4 In the cellar there was a strong _____ of gas.